Life Expressions

By
Sherrita Harrison

Life Expressions
ISBN 978-1-7325036-4-9

Copyright © 2019 Sherrita Harrison

Request for information should be addressed to:
Curry Brothers Marketing and Publishing Group
P.O. Box 247
Haymarket, VA 20168

All rights reserved. No part of this publication may be reproduced, stored in a retrieval system, or transmitted in any form or by any means, electronic, mechanical, photocopy, recording, or any other, except for brief quotations in printed reviews, without the prior permission of the publisher.

Life Expressions

By
Sherrita Harrison

Dedication

I dedicate this book to God who has inspired me many early mornings. To my children Whitney and Brandon whom are my heat beats which generates my blood. To my Mother for all her love, care and support.

Table of Content

Dedication	4
The Tears From My Eyes	7
You Hurt Me	8
Foregiveness Ain't Free, But it's Worth it	9
Love	10
I have the right to remain silent	11
Blessings	12
My Dearest Paul	13
History	15
I'm Sorry	16
Brandon	17
Whitney	18
Mother	19
Father	20
The Best Things in Life Are Free	21
Respect	22
Seasons	23
Your Season is Up	24
You Left Me Uncovered	25
I've Changed My Mind	26
The Lies You Tell	27
Trust	28
I Have A Non-Stick Anointing	29
Don't Answer Your Critics	30
Don't get even, get healed	31
Lies	32
My Man	33
Knowing What To Ignore	34
I Shall Never Let Go	35

My Past Has Passed..36
You Get Mad Too Easy..37
Christians..38
Forgieness Doesn't Make Me A Fool........................39
Don't Try To Mold Me..40
You're Marinating in Your Mess...............................41
You Talk Too Much..42
Woman..43
Black or White..44
I'm Living With A Man That I Can't Stand...............45
How I Let Go..46
I Can't..47
Harvest..48
Faith..49
Failure...50
My Past Isn't Pretty..51
Let Go And Let God..52
Family..53
Travel..54
Your Unhappiness Is Not My Fault.........................55
They Dismissed Jesus..56
People Are Hungry...58
About The Author..61

"The Tears From My Eyes"

The tears from my eyes show a heart that has been broken
The tears from my eyes has a heart that's a token

These tears show fear, anger, and love
Praying for guidance that can only be given from up above

Hearts that are broken can definitely be mended
Tears that are strolling must certainly be ended

If there is anything that I can do to improve this
Please let me know and don't let this be an opportunity missed

The tears from my eyes so desperately want things to be improved
The tears from my eyes says that this mountain can be moved

For my patience is thin and my time is growing short
And the tears from my eyes desires times like the start.

But it's apparent that you really don't care
As I look at you with this flat blank stare

The tears from my eyes are because of you my friend
These same tears from my eyes make me know that this is the end.

"You Hurt Me"

From the first day we met I was apprehensive
Didn't want to be bother. Feeling that my time was too expensive

Not thinking that I was better than you, but thinking ok here we go again
Here is another man that wants to be more than just a friend

Spending time to get to know me was ideal at first
Until you changed with volatility and anger outbursts

You hurt me with lies, trickery, and games
Acting jealous, envious, and making me feel ashamed

Demanding that I wear this and don't wear that
Knowing full well you were playing a game of pity pat

Promising to be the man of my dreams
False promises from start to finish it seems

You hurt me this time but there will be no next
When you finally realize I'm gone and I'm already your ex

So goodbye and so long, I'll cherish the lessons that I've learned
Brought lessons are some of the best lessons ever earned

"Forgiveness ain't free but it's worth it"

He hurt me, so I hurt him back
Just didn't know that my actions would cause such an Attack

Not physical but certainly mental
The overwhelming thoughts and feelings sometimes makes me emotional

I wish I could turn the hands of time
To right the wrong that I've done in my prime

I've cried and prayed that he would forgive me
But didn't see much relief until God set me free

You see I learned how to pray and seek God for myself
It required me to continuously pray and pick my bible up off the shelf

God said in His word that that if I repent with my heart
He provide me forgiveness and peace as He does His part

I learned how to trust God to stand on His word
And for this I have many testimonies unheard

You see I've learned that forgiveness ain't free
But God has given us everything that we want and need

"Love"

Love is patient, kind, and true
Loves allows me to to see and understand you

Understand and love you just as you are
No matter how close or no matter how far

Love covers a multitude of sins
Even when I feel that this relationship won't win

Love allows me to be vulnerable with you
Because you're my man and have proven it too

You see I had to put down my fears and open my heart
So God could allow you to do your part

To find the woman you've been praying for
God opened our hearts allowing us to love once more

Joining together to wed in holy matrimony though rich or poor
Hand in hand walking through open doors

Love allows us to take this journey together
Loving one another unconditionally makes us better

"I have the right to remain silent"

When people boast about the things that they have done
I have the right to remain silent
Because that's a battle that they have already won

When people are obnoxious and speaking loud
I have the right to remain silent
Not stooping to their level makes me proud

When their actions don't match the words that they speak
I have the right to remain silent
Because God's approval is all that I seek

See the Bible reminds us to pray without ceasing
So everything does not require a response that is not pleasing

Continue to pray and God will give us the words to say
That will help us to show others that His commands we must obey

But until we receive directions from God
We have the right to remain silent
To gain His approval and applause

"Blessings"

The water continues to flow
The flowers will continue to grow

The trees will change their leaves
The wind will bring about a breeze

Th sun will shine so bright
As the moon will provide light at night

The ocean will continue to feed
The animals will too after they bleed

Vegetation will have its own season
God is in control for all of the right reasons

He's worthy to be praised
And His commandments must be obeyed

Remember to serve Him and serve Him well
Or wake up after death in eternal hell

There are times that we may make Him weep
But His promises He will certainly keep

God loves us before we even knew how to love ourselves
And because of this I am compelled
To share the gospel through poems and tells

May God Continue To Bless You All!!!

"My Dearest Paul"

*I will never forget
That sunny day that we met*

*Your looks were intriguing
As I pictured you singing*

*Singing a song filled with love
From your heart and your head straight from above*

*But as I got to know you better
My mind seemed more intrigued and wetter*

*Wetter because you watered me with you knowledge
For a single moment I thought I was back in college*

*You helped me to read and grow spiritually
Opening my eyes to things that I could not see*

*I must say that as we began this ship
I did not feel equally equipped*

*To give my heart to another man
But as you see that wasn't God's plan*

*I resisted and fought trying to avoid the inevitable
As God continued to answer the prayers of the credible*

*Creditable man that he sent in my life
Teaching me how to cope with difficulties and strife*

This ship that we are both in
Has been a Godsend and has allowed us to grow past just being friends

So now as our relationship grows
Together we seek God because He's the only one who knows
He knows the purpose and plans that he has
For the both of us to be a part of His serving class

Teaching others God's Word is what we will do
Joined in matrimony tried but true

True and faith to the word of God
Meeting His approval with an applaud

So again I say I'll never forget
Meeting my dearest Paul with no regrets

"History"

As I grew up and went to school
I learned that American History is not that cool

There are some beliefs that a very young man
Discovered this land that was already in hand

The hands of some who trusted him and his crew
Until they found out that they were miscued

I also read about racism, hatred and innocent killings
People were hated because their skin tone had more melanin

Separated by ignorance, race creed, and color
Not knowing that their father slept with some of their women making them brothers

Denying their rights to vote and use the same water faucets and bathrooms
Just made more room for the stupidity to groom

So today as we read our history books
It allows us an opportunity to take a closer look

A look at History, Know and understand
That were given a partial view from only one race of man

The History that we read is simply a version of "His Story"

"I'm Sorry"

It is with greatest regret that I say to you
That I can no longer be that one for you

The one you cherish to have and hold
As you loving wife, I've became quit cold

Cold because my needs were not being met
Thinking back and having some regret

Nonetheless I can admit to my faults
What the years have shown me and taught

Taught me some things that I can do better
In the next marriage as I write you this letter

I'm sorry that I couldn't love you like you wanted
Because of my actions I have sometimes been haunted

Haunted by some things that I've done in my past
But after asking you and God for forgiveness, the feelings didn't last

So again I say that I'm sorry for not being able to truly love you
I'm learned from my actions and my feelings are true

"Brandon"

I prayed that God would bless me with a son before you were ever born
When I found out you were a boy, I sounded the horn

Calling everyone with excitement and joy
Patiently waiting until June to meet my baby boy

You entered the world with the presence of a king
Taking your first breaths, lighting up the room as you sing

Singing a song with tears streaming from your eyes
My heart filled with joy as I gaze at my new prize

You've always had a strong personality since birth
Standing strong and proud on God's green earth

You have a natural talent to play football
Teaching momma the sport as I listen to the calls

It's so interesting to watch you grow up, becoming a young man
As you are learning to take great strides and stands

Always remember to keep God first in this journey through life
And He will guide you through your heartache, trouble, and strife

"Whitney"

To my daughter Whitney so kind and sweet
I couldn't wait until God allowed us to meet

Looking at you for the very first time
Thanking God for making you all mine

As I rubbed you little hands and held you in my arms
Kissing your soft cheeks and keeping you warm

I thank God for showing me the way
To become a mother on this April day

Learning how to parent from trial and error
Making mistakes and sometimes feeling terror

Laughing at little cute things that you did
As you laughed, run, played, danced and hid

The truest blessings is seeing you grow
Obtaining your goals each one you know

I pray that God continues to bless you in this life
As you continue to grow and become someone's wife

"Mother"

My mother, beautiful, supportive and strong
Correcting us when we're not right, but when we're wrong

Loving her husband and children to a fault
Writing things down in her secret journal as she thought

Mother was loving, gentle but stern
Showing us all how she really was concerned

She wanted the best for all of her kids
Reminding us about some of the friends we must rid

Teaching us the daily skills of life
Knowing one day that we would be a wife

Cooking and cleaning were just a few things
That mother taught us life would bring

Independence as young girls and boys
Taking care of yourself even putting up your toys

Mother taught the family how to love one another
Taking up for you sister and your brother

But most importantly she taught us to treat people like you want to be treated
And doing what's right, you can never be defeated

"Father"

Thank you for being such an awesome father
When there are men that wouldn't even bother

Marrying my mother with her four kids
Knocking other guys out with their bogus bids

Showing and teaching us about love each day
As you work so hard to make a way

A way to provide for the family that you had
Making the most out of each day, good and bad

After you and mom had one child together
You never made a difference with the other children, never

You were the best father this girl could have ever had
Even when you wouldn't let me have my way and I got mad

So I thank God for sending you in our lives to be our father
Because there are many men that wouldn't have even bothered

I miss you so much daddy you're the first man that I've ever loved
I'm pray you're smiling from Heaven above

"The Best Things In Life Are Free"

Who says the best things in life are free
If they are, that's something that I don't see

If you want to live a life that is nice
Getting an education comes with a high price

Food, clothing and shelter are basic needs
But a price you will pay to obtain these things in deed

Lights, water, gas, phone and cable all cost
You need a career so that you don't get lost

Lost in the thoughts that things are free
Then finding out that their not for you or me

Transportation, entertainment, and dating can be expensive
Especially if you have to do them extensive

So again I ask, who says the best things in life are free
If they do, please send them to me

"Respect"

Respect is something that most people desire
To get noticed from others or even get hired

Respect should be free but it comes with a price
Sometimes you've got to bite your tongue and be nice

Respect should be given to young and old
Handed to others without limits I'm told

Respect is taught from generation to generation
Passing through this land and great nation

Respect requires letting others know
What will and will not work or things that can't go

Respecting others comes easy to some
But others play like or they are just simply dumb

So respecting our elders is the least that we can do
To prove our respect tried and true

"Seasons"

Seasons change from winter, spring, summer and fall
Not much remains, nothing at all

The trees will lose the leaves for sure
As children will grab their jackets as the walk out the door

Winter will come and the snow will fall
Angels and snowman being built big and tall

Spring will bring colorful change
Cold and warm weather, that's strange

Many people enjoy the summer heat
Laying on the beach and barbecuing their meat

Fall will come and the time will go back
Allowing everyone to get on track

Seasons change from winter, spring, summer and fall
The best thing to do is to try and enjoy them all

"Your Season Is Up"

I don't regret that warm day we met
Not for one minute, no not yet

I learned so much in this short little time
How relationships are important especially in their prime

Spending time getting to know one another
Laughing and talking about none other

Than learning what we like and don't
Putting up with things that we ordinarily won't

Just to give the relationship a fair try
Before the frustration and saying goodbye

But that didn't work so your season is up
I've had enough to overflow my cup

The lies, jealousy and so many other things
Helped me to realize what this relationship brings

Stress and bitterness and lack of trust too
Understanding that I can't continue to stay with you

Because your season is up

"You Left Me Uncovered"

You left me uncovered because of your anger
You allowed it to hold on and stay and linger

You left me out hear with the wolves prowling
Grazing, looking, talking, and howling

You left me uncovered in this cold and ruthless world
Many guys asking me to be their new girl

They couldn't care less about about your feelings they say
Just the desires to get closer to me on this day

You left me uncovered and my look for you has changed
This relationship has taken a shift and it's completely strange

My feeling for you have shifted it's true
Because you left me in the cold shivering and blue

So my suggestion to you for the very next time
Is to keep you woman covered like she's your dime

If you don't know how to cover your spouse
You need to go into that special place, the Lord's house

Learning how to cover your lady is one of your goals
To keep the relationship spicy, fresh, loving, and whole

"I've Changed My Mind"

*I've changed my mind and decided to move on
Realizing where this relationship has went wrong*

*The newness has died and you've grown quit cozy
Listening to others as they ask questions and be nosey*

*It seems that you've had problems from the very start
Jealous and envious of the men in the mart*

*Also reminding me of the difference in age
Didn't matter to me as long as we were on the same page*

*You wanted me to do things for you
Those same things you refused to do*

*So I've changed my mind and that's my right
Moving on to something greater with depth and height*

*I made great sacrifices for love this is true
But I changed my mind because I realize it's not you*

"The Lies You Tell"

The lies you tell are never nothing nice
The lies that you tell cause trouble, grief, and strife

The lies you tell makes me look at you wrong
Those lies that you tell reassures me that you're not strong

Strong enough to support the weight that I carry
Reassuring me that you're not the man that I need to marry

The lies you tell has pushed me further away from you
They broke the trust because of the things we've been through

You had me believing the lies you told
There was a point that I was 100% sold

Because of the lies you've told our love is no more
You've really hurt me down to my core

So take your lies and keep moving on
Out of my sight you and your lies be gone

I'm moving on with forgiveness deep down in my heart
From the lies you told at the very very start

"Trust"

Trust is something that everyone desires
It is one of the most important things that we require

Trust helps to heal your heart that was broken
Mending that heart that has been choking

Without trust we have no certainty
That we can build a relationship that can be

Full of trust without questions and doubts
That can be fulfilling no in's or outs

A relationship filled with trust provides a great foundation
That captures the attention and makes you walk in formation

Letting your guard down and trusting your heart
Because he's proven to be upstanding from the start

Trust will provide reassurance that's true
To love the one that truly loves you

"I Have A Non-Stick Anointing"

I have a non-stick anointing that was given to me by God
It's something people are afraid of poke and prod

Asking how I received blessings from heaven up above
And wondering why I show others so much love

They say I smile and speak to everyone
Seeking attention from all of their sons

I have a non-stick anointing and don't pay attention to what they say
God has a hedge around me that protects me all the way

He protects me from dangers seen and unseen
Guiding my footsteps from people who are mean

But He requires me to still love them and continue to pray
Until He returns on that glorious day

So I'll keep the non-sick anointing to keep God's command
As I read the Bible and place my hand in His hands

"Don't Answer Your Critics"

*People will talk as much as they please
And often times the talk will make us unease*

*Telling things that they assume and do not know
Just so their story can sound appealing and glow*

*You don't have to answer your critics that's true
As they lie and say false and unfavorable things about you*

*I know it's hard to listen to their lies
As you climb higher and attempt to rise*

*Don't answer your critics, no not at all
Because they want a show as they watch you fall*

*Instead pray that will God deal with their mess
And He will allow you to pass this great test*

*Because the prayers of the righteous will truly avail
Thanking God that He has allowed you to fly and exhale*

*By not answering your critics, not even one
So that you can do his work as his son has done*

"Don't get even, get healed"

Sometimes people do things that make us upset
Also saying things that they don't know yet

Our first reaction may not be our best one
We have to learn how to react like God's son

Don't get mad; get healed is what I say
This is not easy; no how, no way

Reading your Bible and studying God's word
Will help you heal from the negativity you've heard

It's something we have to continue to try
Again I'll say it's not easy, No Lie

Ask God to remove anything that's unlike Him
Then you start to shine like a giant gem

Because when your healed you can let things go
Learning to love others that have wronged you, you know

Now your focus have shifted to God and His word
Ignoring the mess that you may have just heard

"Lies"

*A lie don't care who or when it's told
They keep coming up new and old*

*A lie is designed to kill and destroy
The reputation of of others with gimmicks and ploys*

*A lie will separate people from one another
They can even separate a sister from her brother*

*A lie can kill a relationship that's good
Making them act like they're from the hood*

*A lie can make you doubt what others say
Or make you question them day after day*

*A lie can cause a riff between friends
Making hardships that never mends*

*A lie is designed to make people hurt or cry
It's unfortunate that some people lie on ones that die*

*If at all possible, please don't lie
On anyone or anything, it's worth a try*

"My Man"

I don't need no man to be my space or in my place
I just want my man to be in my face taking up my space

While he's with you he's looking at me
Disrespecting you my lusting at thee

So tell your man to put his eyes back in his head
Turning all the way around like the walking dead

I can't deal with these disrespectful brothers
Trying to talk to everyone woman and their mother

My man is true and he plays no games
Putting these lame guys to guilt and shame

You see this is what you must understand
I love the one that I call my man

He's the one that God has sent to me
To spend the rest of of lives together and serve thee

Serving God and teaching others
How to become respectful, strong, loving brothers

That's why I love my man

"Knowing What To Ignore"

You need to be aware of the things you should ignore
Especially when messy people bring junk to your door

Don't get distracted by the things that they say
Because it really doesn't matter now no way

Don't waste your time, energy, or money
On people who are bitter, opposite of honey

Don't lose no sleep about people who do you wrong
Read your Bible especially the book of Psalms and the praises they song

You'll wear yourself out trying to please other men
Walking in circles like little cackling hens

Ignore the mess and use your energy to improve your skills
And God will bring people into your life to do His own will

So stay focus and keep a straight face
Because in the end you'll set the pace for this race

"I Shall Never Let Go"

I will never let go of God's unchanging hand
For I am learning to completely understand

That God has a miraculous plan for me
That others will not comprehend when their eyes see

How God has changed this mouthy little girl
Who will minister to others throughout the world

Helping them to gain knowledge of His Word
Bringing them the truth to lands unheard

Allowing them an opportunity to gain salvation
Searching for souls in every nation

Before He returns to call peace on earth
Many will be baptized causing a rebirth

And they too will be on fire
Spreading God's Word with all who desire

To know the truth and never let go
Of God's hand in this dying world that we know

"My Past Has Passed"

My past has passed, its gone away
I'm too happy because it could not stay

I've done some things that I surely not proud of
Knowing full well that God seen my actions from above

So I have some skeletons in my closet for sure
I keep pushing forward trying to close that door

You see my past ain't pretty I must say
But it won't stop my praises, no way, no how

If one of those skeletons just happen to come out
I'll tell them my past is the past no doubt

Because my life has changed and Jesus is my Savior
I look to Him as my one and only true flavor

I'm truly blessed to have to have His saving grace
Making my life new again in this place

My past is the pass and I'm so grateful
That God has delivered me from being so hateful

So I'll leave the past in the past and keep moving on
As I reverence God as He sits on the throne

"You Get Mad Too Easy"

*You get mad over the simplest little things
Not always knowing what life may bring*

*You get mad when you don't get your way
Acting like a small child, day after day*

*Folding your arms and sticking out your lips
Until you get your way putting your hand on your hips*

*You get mad too easy and that's a bad sign
Relationships are about compromise, not yours or mine*

*You get mad too easy and that's too bad
Knowing full well that your behavior is sad*

*Communication is key to resolving any issues
But you get mad and tear up needing Kleenex's or tissues*

*When you learn to talk instead of getting mad
You'll realize that your problems really aren't that bad*

*So I'll encourage you stop allowing things to make you so mad
An understanding and communication that will end up making you glad*

"Christians"

How are you walking with God but still looking at the past
Focusing on negativity and putting people on blast

Talking about hustling, drinking, and drugs
God don't uphold current gangsters and thugs

Popping your fingers, singing and dancing
But on Sunday mornings you're in church prancing

How you gonna be a Christian with limited knowledge about God
Struggling with your beliefs but perfecting you bod

Trying to get the attention of anyone who cares
Doing things that you shouldn't because of dumb dares

Having intercourse because she has a nice body
Knowing that she's not the only woman who you call a hotty

How do you call yourself a Christian without knowing Christ
Wearing diamonds and pearls from a jeweler's heist

Don't you know that God sees everything
And He knows what your life will bring

So make the changes to live a life that's right
Serving God with all of your might

"Forgiveness Doesn't Make Me A Fool"

Time after time you've done your little dirt
Asking for forgiveness after your actions stabbed and hurt

Hurt the ones you say that you love
Not carrying out the the commands that God gave from above

There has been so much resistance
Which makes me love you from a greater distance

Because I forgive you it doesn't make me a fool
It just allows me to know that you're obnoxious and cruel

Forgiving you is like a golden rule
It only allows me to use my other tool

The Bible commands us to forgive one another
Even the lies you tell on your sisters and brothers

Forgiveness is like taking my hand out of a fire
So I can live life as God so desires

Forgiveness is not for you, you see
It's so I can live the life that God has given me

Walk In FORGIVENESS

"Don't Try To Mold Me"

Don't try to mold me into who you want me to be
Can't you see how God made me

He put man to sleep and took one of his ribs
So that He can form woman with witty ad libs

Don't try to mold me into who you want me to be
Because God made me in His own imagine you see

Strong and mighty loving and caring
Willing to sacrifice by giving and sharing

Don't try to mold me into who you want me to be
God is the Facilitator of life for you and me

He gives us life so that we may live
Loving one another and learning how to forgive

Don't try to mold me into who you want me to be
The Lord almighty has shown mercy on me

So if you want to mold me into who you want me to be
Take your concerns up God the creator of thee

"You're Marinating In Your Mess"

You get upset over the smallest little things
Letting them bother you, disrupting the joy life brings

Marinating in your mess is what you do
Holding on to grudges like a little boy who's two

Talking loud to get attention
Even in school resulting in suspension

Jumping up from the dinner table
Holding a conversation, you were not able

You're marinating in your mess
Instead of talking things out to relieve your stress

When you're being corrected and told that you're wrong
You defend your actions and pretend to be strong

Your actions are truly overrated
Believe me love this is something that I've stated

So stop marinating in your mess and show a bit more concern
This is a great lesson that I hope you've learned

"You Talk Too Much"

You talk too much and that ain't cool
Running around professing Christ but acting like a fool

You talk too much, spreading other people's stories
Like you are a god in all your glory

You talk too much telling this and that
But your story is never up at bat

You talk too much and this is true
Making statements that cause hurt, harm, and blue

You talk too much and it causes problems
So many that you alone can't solve them

You talk too much and this can be scary
Hurting other people including your friend Jerry

You talk to much but you should be quiet
Close your mouth; come on just try it

Because the next time you talk to much, someone just may say
Go sit down with the childish games that you play

"Woman"

Woman stand so proud and strong
As she cares for her family all along

Working two jobs just to keep things together
Keep pressing and moving no matter the weather

Raising little boys to be strong men in this world
Teaching them that boys don't cry like little girls

Telling young girls to be less dependent on others
Leaving little to no errors for the brothers

Not realizing you may be pushing them too much
To be strong and independent never needing a crutch

Someone to love, to have, and to hold
Sharing life with as you grow old

So woman it's great that you love you kids
But arrogance and materialistic wants we must rid

Instead teach your children about our Heavenly Father
Perusing heavenly things and not worldly bothers

"Black or White"

We live in a society that sees primarily black and white
No depth or substance near in sight

Hatred and division is their main goal
To keep others from the truths of things untold

Racial intolerance just because of my skin
Is total ignorance and a deadly sin

Because beneath the surface we all bleed the same
Seeing black and white is so dumb and lame

So embrace diversity and learn about each other
Truth be told we all have the same mother

Eve was the first woman I hope you know
God made her so man wouldn't feel so lonely and low

So get to know people for who they really are
No matter how close, no matter how far

Life is more than black and white
It is about living wrong or right

"I'm Living With A Man That I Can't Stand"

I'm living with a man man that I can't stand
He wants to grab a hold of my hand

He started out a kind gentleman
But turned out to be much more than

More than I could stand in a man
Insecure as he watched me as I ran

Ran from one place to another
Looking and lurking like a stalking brother

So I'm living with a man that I can't stand
Having regrets that I took his hand

I use to love him without fail
Now I can't stand to be around his tail

So I realize that I must go
Before this relationship turns into a show

I'll leave this place with respect
Because I've learned how to disconnect

"How I Let Go"

Sometimes you just have to let go and let God
Especially when things are not right and they're odd

Take your hands off of it and learn to pray
Ask God for His will on this blessed day

But He can't move if you're trying to handle it on your own
Get out of you feelings because of the seeds that were sown

Let go and let God deal with things as He May
Allow you to see vindication as you stay

Stay on your knees asking Him to intercede
Praying fervently as you petition and plead

Just remember that God doesn't move by our clock
His timing is impeccable; solid as a rock

He makes no mistakes and need no help
Because all of your prayers He's heard you yelp

So let go and let God fight the battle at hand
He's won more fights than any other man

"I CAN'T"

I can't deal with this no more
Every time a black man walks out the door

We never know if he's coming back
Because some trigger finger cop just might attack

Shooting unarmed men left and right
This is senseless and getting out of sight

Sandra Bland's murder was covered up
Cops lying more frequently y'all need to wake up

She was just one of so many
Murdered in cold blood like they weren't any

Murdered like they didn't belong
To anyone as they were wronged

They're life cut short because of ignorance and hate
We need a solution before it's too late

Because I can't sit back as they continue to kill
Getting their rocks off and all the cheap thrills

"Harvest"

You can't have harvest without sowing seeds
Whether it's sowing good or bad deeds

Lending a hand to one another
Helping your sisters and your brother

Speaking positive things into their life
And not condemning them because of their strife

Keep building them up and never tearing them down
Showing them support all the way around

Because you can't have harvest with sowing seeds
There is not one single person that doesn't have needs

So if we care and love each other
We will assist all the children from our mother

Sowing seeds that will take strong roots
And when it's harvest time we will need our boots

To plow the fields that are good and plenty
So we can assist others with any

Anything that they have a need
Because we have planted those good seeds

"Faith"

*The Starting Point of Faith is fear
We have to trust God even through the tears*

*Without fear we wouldn't have any belief
That God will help us and give us some relief*

*So we choose faith over fear
Because God carries us far and near*

*The Bible tells us that about faith in the book Hebrews
Trusting in God is something we can't lose*

*When we practice faith we may not see
What God is doing for you and me*

*Faith requires work according to the book of James
That includes everyone, no specific names*

*Faith carries us places that no man can
Because our lives are in God's hands*

*So if you've learned anything at all
Trust in God, He will never let you fall*

"Failure"

Failure is not the end
From your failures you can mend

Failures allows us an opportunity to grow
Failures help us to learn and know

How to overcome those failures in fact
So they won't have a lasting impact

On our lives and keep us from moving on
Because failure helps us to grow and be strong

When we fail, we get back up
Come back stronger with our cup

Cup of knowledge from the last time we failed
With the willpower to prevail

To try again but in a different way
Persistence pays off we will see one day

And on that day we can rest ashore
That particular failure will be no more

We conquered that one now on to the next
Checking the box after reading the text

"My past isn't pretty"

My past isn't pretty and I cannot lie
There are some skeletons that refuse to die

People try to bring them back alive
But that don't work because they're full of jive

Everyone has things that they're not proud of
Don't think you're better because God sees you from above

He sees our past and hears us repent
Allowing us to move forward with the angels he sent

I'll leave my past in the past with the intent to be strong
Not looking back at the things I've dong wrong

Praying for forgiveness and change of heart
Thanking God for allowing me to have a new start

Each day I'll give Him the honor and praise
For teaching and showing me my hands I raise

I raise my hands to God be the glory
Sharing this message by telling my story

No My past isn't pretty, but I'll let the past stay in the past
And allow God to deliver me so I will be free at last

"Let Go And Let God"

Some people hold on to things that have hurt them in their past
With both hands clinched like its their last

Their last breath that they'll ever breathe
Not realizing in their lives they have grieved

Taken on the baggage of not letting go
Stress weighing you down, that's a no no

So let go and let God have His way
Then you can have relief and live another day

Live to serve and do God's will
Releasing you of stress and taking all kind of pills

When you let go and let God, He'll straighten your path
Solving all problems like doing the math

Trust in God, and do your best
Give your troubles to Him and He'll do the rest

Let go and let God and He'll resurrect you from the tomb
Giving you new life like you're fresh out of the womb.

"FAMILY"

I was born into this family of which I love
Spared by Jesus who came from above

Giving us life to live at free will
But understanding at the end, you've got to pay the bill

So as my parents raised us, they told us right
Do things decent and in order with all of your might

Treat people how you want to be treated
Speaking kindly to others is how they shall be greeted

Tell the truth and don't you lie
Lies you won't keep up with even with an alibi

Help one another in any way that you can
Strengthen your brother and fellow man

Forgive one another for their downfalls
You cannot judge, that's not your call

I was born into this family who taught me great things
Showing me how to have morals and values in this life as it brings

"TRAVEL"

As I travel I see new things
Enjoying what this life brings

It gives me hope and diversity
As I embrace uncertainties

Tasting foods from different states
Hoping one day to meet my soul mate

As I travel to and fro
I've learned to take God as I go

Acknowledging Him before I set out
Taking my Bible without a doubt

Viewing God's beautiful land
That He has created with his miraculous hands

Standing in awe of the stars and the moon
As I sat and ate ice cream with a small spoon

So I just want to take some time to say
Lord I thank you for making a way

"Your Unhappiness Is Not My Fault"

It's unfortunate that so many people are unhappy
Belittling others and making them feel crappy

They walk around with their head hung down
Sometimes gazing and staring as they wear a frown

Talking about people that they don't like
Because they're different, their hair may be spiked

Your unhappiness is not my fault
It's something that I've been taught

If I want to be happy, I have to do what pleases God
Learning to keep His commandments here and abroad

Loving and helping those who are in need
God notices our actions and all of our deeds

So encourage one another to do His will
And you'll soon feel like you've taken a healing pill

No, your unhappiness is not my fault
But I want to show you the love that I was taught

"They Dismissed Jesus"

He came down to earth to give His life
As a living sacrifice for our strife

Some accepted Jesus but others did not
Their rage increased as their tempers ran hot

They questioned Him being the son of God
As they persecuted, poked, punched and prod

They called Him everything but His name
As they continued to point fingers with shameless blame

But Jesus continued to fulfill His mission
As He faced hate and opposition

He prayed to His father that all may see
The will of God which is priceless because it's free

But that didn't stop some from doing evil deeds
Forgetting about their family and their needs

Jesus took their ridicule relentless in stride
As He continued to seek God with no pride

Then one day some decided to kill Him because they didn't believe
That He was the son of God who came to relieve

They tortured Jesus and nailed Him to the cross
Enraged with hate, their minds were loss

As Jesus hung high He continued to pray
That God forgive them for their behavior on this day

When our Savior took His last breath
They thought that was the end with His death

But early one morning He rose my friend
Ascending to heaven taking the throne once again

"People Are Hungry"

People are hungry and not being fed
Going to church but their spirit is still dead

The Preachers lips are moving telling all kinds of lies
Scaring people about hell with their wicked ties

Whooping and hollering from the church's pulpit
In a chair is where their butt should sit

Taking up money for their own personal gain
Wanting the parishioners to attend church even through their pain

Trying to increase their church's attendance and offerings
Showing no real concern to the people's true sufferings

Preachers preying on the parishioners, it's sad
People watching the preacher's actions that have gone bad

Wake up people because you're not being fed
Read and study your Bibles to get your own bread

God will give you everything you need
Open His Word and do take heed

It'll will resolve any problem that one may face
Just take the time to read the Bible any time any place

*God will reward everyone who adheres to His Word
Trust and believe Him are the the two best things that I've heard*

*Then the people won't be hungry because the Word will have feed
Leading you to a righteous life so you won't end up spiritually dead*

About the Author

This collection of poems was revealed during various moments in my life. Sherrita M. Harrison is the author of the Life Expressions series. She share spiritual and intimate poems about things that she has encountered and overcome.

Got an idea for a book? Contact Curry Brothers Marketing and Publishing Group, LLC. We are not satisfied until your publishing dreams come true. We specialize in all genres of books, especially religion, leadership, family history, poetry, and children's literature. There is an African Proverb that confirms, *"When an elder dies, a library closes."* Be careful who tells your family history. Are their values your family's values? Our staff will navigate you through the entire publishing process, and take pride in going the extra mile by exceeding your publishing goals.

Improving the world one book at a time!

Curry Brothers Publishing, LLC
PO Box 247
Haymarket, VA 20168
(719) 466-7518 & (615) 347-9124
Visit us at www.currybrotherspublishing.com

www.ingramcontent.com/pod-product-compliance
Lightning Source LLC
Chambersburg PA
CBHW052117070526
44584CB00017B/2534